HEART SEED

For Ray & Donna
Thank you for loving political
poetry — Enjoy this book
& resist!   ♡ Dan

Heart Seed

OAK CHEZAR

When Womyn Made Fire Press

"We die. That may be the meaning of life. But we do language. That may be the measure of our lives." (Toni Morrison)

"They tried to bury us, not knowing we were seeds. "
(Mexican proverb)

These poems are for Mama Earth, and Her protectors.

CONTENTS

~ One ~

THE PROMISE

To be responsible
means to promise in return
To whom is this promise made
and in return for what?
What is the source of your life?
As children we swallowed indigestible lies
that tied us to lifetimes of denial
paradise reduced to a world where
we produce and consume more of everything
but you can tell a child anything
and what we really are
is a seedbed
for the future
feeding
on the grief of the present

To whom are you responsible?
What is the source of your life?
They told us we can live without earth and air,
rivers, trees, animals
but we need to grow up

and we Promised in return
the choice is ours —
will we learn to listen to other voices?
Can we sprout this stump to a tree of Revolution?
Can we jump like the pump in the heart of evolution?

Cos inspiration never left us here alone and
creativity's just been wanderin' around
waiting for us to wake up and come on home
We are pieces of ancient earth
bits of sacred story soaked in intellect and dirt
flowing with time's river

Beyond the daily data fed to us by liars
lies the wind
and inside it's spin swings the chrysalis
in a future forest world
endlessly branching like questions I can imagine
and under the branches, we're seeds in the ground
crouching
ready to change the world again
To whom are you responsible?
What is the source of your life?

This is not a metaphor, friends
let's be butterflies
re-entering, wet and tender
let's drop it all
and pick up one thing at a time
You can't do anything with your life
that you can't first imagine in your mind
I'm not ready to bring down civilization
but I'm ready to imagine it

Let's just walk away
or stay and smash the state
Let's liberate grace
with a fuse and a match
let's hatch out in time to fall
into fields of life and give back
We work from the fringes
from the fertile growing edges
We're shapeshifters
turning from this lost and lonely shore
we are humans, returning
and we're older than war

~ Two ~

THE UNDERGROUND

After a workshop on *Taking Down Civilization*
bouncing off firewalls and barbed wire
for 3 days
and losing
everything
I walk into the woods
the trees take me
bite
by bite
late May green shines
on all the stories told so far
in so many voices
our questions braiding into silence
generations of humans
splitting atoms
splitting eves
budding trees hypnotize the high prairie sky
full of daylight
hiding flowers of starfields for later
and — (you know this) —
we need a different ending

Empty your pockets of impossible wishes

this culture won't shift without a shove
and i've hidden my longing
to hand myself over to this land that's learned me so well
carbon-based primitive
in a silicon world
But i can name green unfurling kites
of willow, dogwood, alder, aspen
Memory coded by spaces and shapes
head stuffed full patterns, rituals
revolutionary strategies
tactics of the underground
teach me to be
the fulcrum, the pivot
and the fuse

I want to be your servant, Life
I been keening a spiral song
junkyard dog orbiting a rusting stake
wearing a circle
at the end of steel links
pacing
till i drop the chain on bare earth
with the grass all worn away
rush into the fray
sword drawn
arrive.

Time of thick cocoons stretched like bats
hung between flowering sticks
heavy with spring thumping life
and i can feel my tail stronger now
my heart wants escape from *the real world*
my guts the guts of an animal

the cocoons' worms work free
sun beats on a thrillion sticky strands
of ten thousand chrysalises
ready to hatch out and eat chokecherry leaves
who are ready to die
to be part of this miracle.

And i was ready to die already
but no such luck
sucked back in
with so much work to do
caterpillar rises to devour what she can reach
What can i reach?
Arms and heart extended
tiniest toeholds calling me to act
what physics of devotion to bring
which furious silver waters
down like who's blessing?

The three teachers split us into groups,
posed simple questions
How To Stop Them, in many iterations
and off we were sent to midwife answers
(so sure of our minds' power to find answers)
blasted down from heights
we laddered our unhinged minds to climb
girders of imagination, scaffolds of daring
our hugest unmasked urgencies
beating a clock inside and outside
our fragile activist bodies

and nothing
nothing to stop them

as the world dies all day long while we reach to stop them
creatures, land bases, air, water die
For 3 days we reached and flung our spirits
high as we could
got hung up there
part of me up there dangling still
and forever.

Today i'm reaching alone
testing the lever of my own arm and heart
saying Us and meaning it
these trees, this river and me are Us
and it's time to get serious
'cos i been sideways in this world too long--
A greenhouse isn't a garden.
A garden isn't a rainforest.
Unquiet inside as leaves
I go underground in my mind
crawling through darkness
practice pivots in my cells
transformed to winch, assassin, silent vapor
wanna throw the night around my shoulders
throw myself over the loudest rapids of May
yell my life out in one long call
not knowing if what returns
is an answer
or an echo

Moving out, pollen on the winds
from a workshop that shattered certainty
detonating this next level of struggle
wrapped inside a prayer for magic
moving out to defend

geranium, butterfly, bear
new spring leaves in every forest

Thorns on roses glitter
skyscraper of mountain
dares me in vast verticality
to stop them
Tower of trees vibrating messages in code
to pass along, not alone
Stop Them.
coded explosives
viruses uncoil
hurricanes roar through the nests
Stop them! Stop them! Stop them!
Just blood pushing against thought
How many years? How many decades?
How much will be left
when we each finally decide?

My heart turning over and over in the spring-somersaulted air
here is redemption: pay your rent
The how is harder now, the fear more meat
pit of questions shoveled in with brutal details
history and the future converged in that room
a faint current connects us still
like being stuck to an electric fence
neither able to let go nor hold on
simply present
lifted
to be ancestors
of a world where martyr means witness
to take our future place among the incoherent buds
felled in summer drifts beneath the ancient sun

I catch sight of the question limping behind us —
— was it worth it,
the torn-open veins, the brutalized hearts?
One drop of my blood the crimson dew
on every blade of sprouting grass
and I would trade my life for any tree in the forest
so much safety in our world that
safety's become the source of danger
Universities teach the unified theory of nothing
our best youth crawl through those doors
emerge contaminated
greedy, indebted & numb
completing that journey
begun with one
bright
green
breath

By the awakened river
broken spruce sprouts a new crawl of trunk
pumps out cerise nipple cones
breath stacked in stones:
red-green-red-green-
it's all code i crack between aging teeth
Moss waits years to exhale
and begin again
I step into the form of fighter
again
familiar archetype
like river, chrysalis, evergreen
life's a rolling explosion
if you're awake

truth smashes into you like an iceberg
and even if your heart's built like a Mayan pyramid
you go down
haunted by lost things with false stories whispering
i want.. i want..
I bed down most night, satisfied with this life
while the lichens lie down
in defiance of gravity
how to press into home like that
heart-first to stone?
Mother, lover, lie down with me like this
tap coded victory stories out of my bark
let it flow like maple syrup into pails
squeeze me till it all comes out sweet
and true

Building warrior culture
with buds of books
with spring words, summer words
to keep the people warm in winter
Give me my muse
and a passion that does not pass
this is my chance
to climb through the flames till i am the fire
smooth as a tube to listen through
what old land is calling?
Decipher messages of ancestors
not necessarily mine
a chorus of voices asking
how far down can one person reach
from the edge of too late
towards the luminous bones

of that forgotten home

Spring 2011

~ Three ~

CORNOGRAPHY

The Mayan people believed they were made of corn
Through the storms of history they prayed to the gift and the
mystery
    whispered into the open ears of maize
Now their descendants buy Kraft instant corn that's GMO
and Walmart sells the most tortillas in Mexico
and the seeds are patented by Monsanto

While on this side of the border
high fructose corn syrup rules our religious order
A million acres aching under the weight of corn syrup
—a sacrifice to CocaCola
Our food pyramid keeps rolling over
like dice on a craps table betting our food security
like crops under the combine of oil and soiled chemistry
We grow bigger with agribusiness
forcing trade agreements that are slave agreements
U.S. corn fired through the weapon of NAFTA
the final solution of those corporate bastards, our masters
in a world full of farmers smashed flat by the power of one
Conquest is done without guns these days
as corn conquers the earth in an industrial haze

In the whorehouse of Free Trade, the first task
is prostituting all that surplus biomass
It's not just soda pop, check out the meat
USDA's plan is to shove as much corn as they can
into the guts of the animals that we eat
Shape-shifting them to *production units* like they never had a heart
Served up to us boneless and bloodless as a poptart
More fossil fuel machines
but these are able to suffer
Feeding corn to cows, chickens, even salmon
'cos farm policies champion this crop and no other
They subsidize high fructose corn syrup, but not carrots
so the cheapest calories in the supermarket
are also the unhealthiest

Barcoded, irradiated, genetically amalgamated
CORN— the biotic army of one, replacing all others
Mothers blinded by the plastic shine
infinite horizons of monoculture
A global tide of homogenization
now they've liberated food from nature
This corn was re-born of the machine
weaning us off real nutrition to a new cuisine
We're eating more of a single plant than Life ever dreamed of

The food chain's tentacles are transcendentical
Longer and longer and less comprehensible
Many different shapes, but the food's all identical
Perishable, like instincts traded for antibiotics
We're sipping petroleum in a culture made neurotic
but it's time to get real

Cos we're like cows in a feedlot laying in their own shit
and that shit served back to them, bit by bit
We're like veal
We're like chickens or pigs squealing for mercy from the cages
to the slaughter line
the last page of their miserable corn-stuffed life
You are what you eat
We stand in lines, conquered by monotony
We eat what they toss in the trough
numb to the cacophony
My people stumble along
pretending not to hear the pop!pop!pop!
of the stun-guns song

And it comes down like a hammer
right between the eyes
And we drown, and we act surprised
like disease is a failure of medicine
and not the heart of this heartless system
that grades us all according to cuts
and how well we fit as production units
Spraying poisons and patents
monopolies and cancer
corn is laundering money for Cargill and Con Agra

But wherever you live, the sun falls for free
and life turns itself into food for you, willingly
It's all a garden we've been taught not to see
If we could tear down the walls
and watch our foodsheds disappearing
If we could tear ourselves away
from the bright lights and jingles that we're hearing
If we could starve the corporations in this fast food nation

that have conquered the landscape and drained all imagination
To trade the logic of nature for the logic of industry
We're gonna see how it turns out that convenience is the enemy
We've forgotten how to pray to food anymore
but my body is a temple to corn
Corn.

~ Four ~

DREAM OF A SEED

For 400 thousand generations
humans lived at nature's speed
until now

Technology ran all other options out of town
lied about the possibilities, and burned the whole house down
Ripped off from the ground you found
you been taken hostage by the electronic mob
surrounded by mirrors of digital throb
Incarcerated shells in high tech cells
just business as usual here in hell
Society reshaped without our permission
centralized command & control
every empire's mission

The process itself overpowering all doubt
Even if you had the time
you don't have the language
to protest progress
to ask who benefits
you know that the real gift's for industry and military
it was never for us
still you jump on the internet like its some bus

to somewhere real
You say
I just use it to get information
and your masters say
that's right —
get in formation!

They got ten thousand devices, the interlocking whole
tumblers click into locks, cocked and ready to roll
hardware and software, the social crutch
have any people ever been so sure about so much?
Machines extend you, hurled down digital rails
swung from shining infrastructures off one fingernail
dazzled while electric fields multiply
& burning white glitches tear holes in the sky

You carry disposable devices as if they'll save your lives
not seeing how they've taken over
what's left of your lives
and you never ask the most radical questions
Why
have you become this metabolized?

Reptile brain caught in the light from the screens
evolution sits in darkness unable to dream
your senses denied, you're colonized
by repetition ritualized
becoming less like animals, that's the consequence
confirming nature's irrelevance
your kids are leashed to their rooms by cords
Nature's perfection just makes em bored
imaginations caged, bleeding to death
while intangible ghosts suck their last breath

their mama's a global commodification
their daddy's electromagnetic radiation
indoctrination starts early for The People of the Screen
even the children, part whore & part slave
everybody pickin' virtual cotton
in the digital plantations of cyberspace

But I was born half a million years ago
when the earth was sanctified
communities situated in space & time
I wanna wake every kid to what he knows is true
before you put a Playstation into his hands, he knew
we're just dreams of seeds, pulse of beasts
we're shadows cast by clouds
and the roots lying underneath
murmuring on the other side of all this buzzing brightness
woven into our animal memories
before the great loneliness

Stop teaching kids science till you've taught em Connection
love of earth, not a smooth silver tube of rejection
time to end this trance so they can transcend
let them dance till their senses catch fire again
snake their roots deeper till they hit pulsing strata
life wants wings, not weights, the fake gravity of data

There are dragons sleeping under the wired earth
guarding the treasure of blood and breath
one blue-green seam of light, barely breathing
one red thread pumps ecstasy and meaning
This is the war between flesh & drones
machines vs. air, fire, water, and stone
heaps of broken symbols chant your uncaging

you fly out of your boxes enraged and enraging
now it's safe to shut off yr devices
go deaf to the tones
the open secret of nature suffices
still dreaming poems
your Soul's dialing in
fucking hang up the phone.

~ Five ~

THE MUSHROOM MESSIAH

we wake shaking
breathless witness to our melt-down
as coastlines drown
this empire breaks down
& we send our minds
into the cloud
like dandelion seeds
while
down there
in the wheelhouse darkness
eminent domain of molds & bacteria
holds court
forever

Whoever makes up a story, makes up a world.

here's a story
just in time
of never-ending leaf-fall
all the composted years

and all the leaves to come......

once upon a time
before our un-knowable future
before History was another word for Irony
horrors of conscious extinction unrolling
as wars hammer us down
evolution flexes all our frames
& empties the water
from our burning house
beneath monster imposters of illumination
gadgets and greed
chewing on bombast and gristle
lives an Old Story
so new it's still in the middle of unfolding and
i stand in the echo of failed human
above everything that made everything
and everything that unmakes it
chanting
All hail the holy fungus!

no dividing and conquering
just comfort and support
for every verdant unfoldment
each blue wave riding a green world
we bow our flower bodies
across flashing eons
of rusting guns and cracked concrete
seedlings sprouting through eye-holes
and ribcages
what if
all our misery sets the stage
for the coming

of The Mushroom Messiah?

— problem solver extraordinaire—
collaborating with all creation
blind mimes mesmerizing
invisible splayed-out universes
healing the world from trauma
balancing every forest
silently
all consequences just food for them
holding Life in their mysterious hearts

born to share with the great forest trees
one living fractal
threadlike masses networking
moving
so
slowly
on ....
benevolent spores
whose ancient basement rooms
pulse with cosmic demolition crews
all set to begin again
every fantasy egg ready to crack
now

o mycellium!
caregivers of life —
reciting all possibilities like multiplication tables
down there in the endless storied underground
don't need oxygen or sunlight so
they've lived with earth the longest
survived every other Great Extinction

are indigenous deeper than anyone
looking for a solution?
fuck technological innovation
follow that fungus!

through every mass extermination
they played horns in the subterranean orchestra
drummed while ice covered the earth
predicted the dinosaurs' crash with their cymbals
played silvered flutes to sulfur-spewing volcanoes
tinkled extinct ivories of Chernobyl and Fukushima
like a whistle about to blow
waiting
the bow held just above the strings
down there
poised above our despair
weaving strategic fairy looms
they're mapping Gaia's future

they took notes on the big bang
memorized the fractal face of god
are lit inside their deep darkness with memories
and remedies
for shit we haven't even imagined
(yet)
imagine now--
patient
waiting through mutations
facing down toxifications
knowing the holy words or what passes for words
sliding from spaces that pass for mouths
every mouthful, a renaissance
servants of synergy

humming songs of global warming
another climactic cataclysm, but
these schisms are nothing but lunch to them

fasten yr seatbelts, 2-leggeds
'cos here comes the end of our brief stay
of poetry and industrialization
farming and fighter jets
evolution pitching out a zillion guesses per second
all endings beginnings
in the great rolling hula hoop
nesting unseen below breath
— who knows where they came from or where they're going? —
just call Them *Mother*
and trust that this is way deeper than we are

once upon a world
there was a vast *presence*
and no religions are made in its image
a magic carpet of life
slow-waltzing without end
and so
darkness spangled with Life survives
eternally creating forests and babies
from garbage and greed
no scams or nasty side-effects
just act upon act
piled high on a cosmic plate
gobbling all consequences
— relax.
the smooth stalk digests all karma
and out slides the next sacred thing

The Mushroom Messiah
picking up the check for our table
where
i leave my tip
— a poem —
   and
   wait
with an open heart
  to be taken,
  sighing,
  down

For Paul
Stamets

~ Six ~

THE RAPTURE

In the beginning there was relation
In the end there's fear and separation
Just the toll our soul takes, it's the shaking away
from the only god there ever was
The MotherGod — Nature
Patriarchy makes us hate her
Declares war on earth, says we're sinners from birth
divided and blinded we stumble unminding past
all the extinctions required by the eye in the sky
Religion — filling the till
Religion — killing free will
Until we believe the bribes and the lies
that god is a man
that heaven is all he wants us to want
so everyday
he deepens the spell of hell down here
If this patriarchy ain't hell
it's the lobby or nearer —

Glass houses of megachurches hurling stones
Evangelicals droning at suburban clones
SUV's in parking lots lined up like tombstones

Worshipping outer space
where heaven waits
to annihilate earth.

We live in an anti-renaissance
the final act of imperialism
jizzin
all over the body spread out on the rack
spasms like a long slow heart attack
The Great Mother, who's started to attack us back

She birthed us and fed us throughout the green vastness of time
Ecstasy's wet nurse
She opened her purse
of DNA mollecules, fabulous rituals
For a million seasons
She planted a billion reasons for life to live
She was makin' Time
Writing songs called Paleolithic, Mesozoic, Neolithic
ages flying by
flipping pages of streaming time
Cells divided in turquoise seas
She spun sunbeams
played in dinosaur dreams
Life made lichens and worms
fishes and birds
Breath merging, herds converging
threads tumbled together
in a web She spun
Sipping oneness through the red straw of our blood and our love
She was working out her slow, unwinding solution
layin down fossils way before mankind's pollution
and—oh — wait

You don't believe in Evolution!

The male god says don't believe in science
says there's no Great Mother
no relation to others
I say this myth of yours
is the source of all the misery, brothers
You're wasting my time
and I'd rather spend it
wasting your creations
I waste them in vindication of the Goddess and Time
Wasting your Humvees, your suburban dreams
your surveillance satellites
your urban blight
Watch me wasting your war-mind
in defense of evolutionary time.

Once upon anti-entropic cycles of biologic time
Deathless star breath inhabited every cell
told us we are mollusks and chlorophyll
iron and carbon
We're memories of wilderness
not the machines of His holy uterus

Before the wars and
their holy book that lied
tried telling us
that we are at the center
That men alone entered
arm in arm with god
Entered armed with god
Entered Paradise bearing weapons to subdue creation
prepared to open fire on green Life's desire

just to live.

This is the end you say
and you fire time —
open fire on Time
You say this is The End Time?
Maybe this is the end of *your* time ruling *our* minds!
YOU!   Who stride alone beside god
Raping nature for the profits of the prophets of this empire that
fires time
    plants nothing but landmines
    that denies biology, erases evolution
    it's tentacles identical to every violent terrorist act
    Changing the sex of god is the first fact
    that brackets the horror-house of history
    His story
    We and the earth are sick to death of his story!
    Shake us awake
    from night stallions of patriarchal epochs
    Take us back
    to milleniums of magnesium,
    calcium, chromium, potassium
    Back
    to the bare bones of our befores

Restore to us the lush green womb
I am Nature
The envy and enemy of modern man
I am the Goddess
the ground of all being
Her beautiful tenacious yes-sing
Yes-sing — the only song she knows
ringing from the boughs of great trees

Bow down!
Put your knees to the ground
and let her pound you full of her good sense
some essence
beyond the dumbing down, fear filled brains
smoothed out to fit into his heaven's gate
No friction — just airbrushed addiction
Like a home-run
sliding into the purity and security
of the final gated kingdom
where the spectator sport of male theology
tells us to shut up and sit down
and keep projecting Satan out there
All evil doers out there
wandering in some wilderness
you haven't blasted through
yet

Listen, man
I don't want your approval!
I want removal
from the society of good Christian men
who batter Christian wives
who rape Christian children
Who steal, cheat, horde, torture
in the name of god
Who's big world view is limited due
to the bullet shattered windows
of Humvees they stare through
Who imagine themselves above everybody else
cos their idiot in chief was re-elected
to reinstate prayer in the bloody schools
and leave these fools their assault weapons on shelves in stores

patriots playin' hero in these culture wars
till U.S. foreign policy mirrors the bible's prophesy
Like the mirrored sunglasses on god's big face
staring back at a haunted race
so afraid of Life
they wanna take   it   out

But you're so wrong —
'cos god is a Mother
and
swirling through Time
from the first cell floating on the first sea
at the first outbreath of the world
that breath still circles
chanting only Yes!
God is a Womin who just says Yes!
and we gotta give Life support saying Yes!
and maybe these death throes are really birth pains
maybe this chaos is labor, not apocalypse
And maybe what we need to do is push—
Push through her hips
Push! Push through.

The end of patriarchy is my rapture
and I ain't goin' nowhere
but Here.

                              2006— The re-election
of GW Bush

~ Seven ~

LADY GADUMPSTADIVER

Part One

I prostrate myself at the bottom of the wet dumpster
It's a form of worship
Exalt praises of glory in the silence of heretics
an act of amends for the crimes of my culture
Listen
you can hear the cosmic applause
back in time
ahead in time
It's the scene of a crime —
discarded apples, strawberries, a bruised peach —
cos anything taken for free in late stage industrial capitalism
is a criminal activity
Stealing, or trespass, breaking, entering
cheating
Cos we're supposed to trade our lives to just BE here
and i just wanna BE Here

And the fact that I'm driving a car is a hypocritical complication
for another poem
    driving with my knees
    cos I got my hands shoved up against heating vents

defrosting frozen fingers that ache as they thaw
from picking the icy dumpster's pockets full of wet produce
and I give thanks for the car, cos i hate cars, but love my car
Paradox — more holy to a hippie than hypocrisy

A produce dumpster's cleaner than you think
No half eaten pizza crusts, no napkins nobody blew their nose on
Just organic produce
flattened boxes, me, maybe some raccoon family
down there in the darkness
I drove down the mountain for this bounty from the world
Climb up, do a modest gymnast's flip and land atop it all
in this frigid winter Boulder dumpster behind Wild Oats
soon to be Whole Foods, on it's way to morph to Amazon
Land boots first on shaky layers separating random, colorful
chaos
I squat to balance on stiff cardboard steps
grab Mexican grown broccoli
organic bundles tied in purple rubber bands
tomatoes from Argentina, apples from New Zealand

Stand here with me and peer down, just follow the light of my
headlamp
There's cantaloupes, ripe and only slightly dented
three boxes of very expensive mushrooms, untouched
seven boxes of asparagus — in December! —No wonder the earth
is melting!
Uneven steps make stages to stand
separate vegetables and fruits into levels
according to archaeological values of time
deposited and waiting
For me.
For you.

Last week
I climbed down into the almost-empty, echoing dumpster
lured by a deep vision of three dozen/ dozen eggs.
Squatting at the bottom, cadaverous, dumbed with dirt like coal
in the earth
wondering at this sacrificial offering from unseen hands, and
how I'm gonna lift these fragile full eggshells up over my 5 foot
3 inch head
and then lower them
to the level of parking lot
on the other side of this tall metal food coffin wall
without smashing the hell out of 'em?

Dude in a black hoodie exits the bright warm store and enters
my world
eclipse of the night
tosses 2 big black plastic garbage bags
into the blind dumpsters' inky corner without looking
They sail up towards the stars, reverse direction, and land
heavy with squish, on top of my crouching form
My glasses pop off my face, land somewhere in darkness among
the eggs
"OW! Fuck, man!"
scaring the living shit out of the produce worker
"Oh my god! I'm so sorry! Are you o.k.?"
he turns back, let's the heavy door slam behind us
"No, i'm not o.k.!"
"Oh, wow — well, what can i do?"
"Just grab these eggs, man.
Help me get 'em outta here."
And he does
I raise boxes up in my hands

an offering to the earth goddess of food rescue
and he receives them from me, a stacked pile at a time
gently sets them on the ground beside my car
over and over
returns to give me a hand out

and
I leave the lot with one black eye
four bunches of asparagus, two cantaloupes, fifteen apples
and one hundred forty-four unbroken eggs
Saved like a Kansas baptist in a river
while he stands there at midnight holding 2 cartons of eggs for
his family
his tip from my endless heathen slush fund
cos you gotta circulate the prosperity
here
in the land of the free
the home of the brave

Part Two

In Garbageland we stand
finding dignity in this wasteland
We refuse the command to control
take refuge in the refuse
Free the contraband
it's all free in no man's land
Private property means
everything's owned
or it's for sale
maybe it's on sale
get it retail, wholesale

get it free

God's portion
Diving past razor blades
making our own mistakes
Done
with the monetary monotony of spending and wasting
All the hungry stores wanting more
My people buy new shit to drive to the dump
they take regular dumps
wanting more
All of it pumped, stabbed, ripped
from the Mother
Civilization takes us all down
Wanting more

We're urban foragers
waste not, want not
Surplus and distressed food
a second harvest, anyone?
Forget about hedge funds, just hop a hedge
Let the small thrills take you
It's a hunter-gatherer renaissance
pre-civilized and post-civilized
Imagine diving into abundance like that
trusting freedom
climbin' in not buyin' in
Just help yourself in The Land of Away
Tearing open that first bag of trash is our first step to freedom

Part Three

Ninety billion pounds of food is wasted every day here

— we just want a little taste —
But these people are so scared to share
they stare through the poor
and put locks on their dumpster doors
Who finds satisfaction
when every transaction
goosesteps to the rules set by money—
You think this rat race is alright, honey?
I say we need a rat strike!
Here, against the masters of production
Now, before disasters of consumption
take us down

So I'm divin in under the command to control
and it's all stolen, but I'm rollin with what's out there
When they clear those market shelves, I'm a garbage elf
poppin the tops off the forbidden boxes
I dance with Pandora
to even the score up
In a culture that defines itself by what it buys
what if I'm not buyin'?

In my dream, we strip Capitalism bare,
leave him tied to a cold radiator, there
in his empty house
remembering Nature
Seize the blade of empire and peel it to the root
live on dumpstered fruit
What if you're not buying?
Imagine diving into the garbage
it's sweeter than you think
Just go round the back of the store
instead of the front door

and you're Free

One stop shopping at the curbs in the burbs
or the alleys of the cities
where everything that sucks about Capitalism
is reversed when you score
Metabolize the sins of
More! More! More!
And dumpster diving is evolution
cos this system can deal with every solution —
protests, elections, terrorism
everything
except for people who ask for less
Let's ask for less

Structurally adjust that
merchants of commerce who never negotiate
World traders who trade the whole holy world
for the beat up rubble, for a blow up bubble
that expands forever in a clever trick
of Viagra economics
But that's astronomic bull
'cos this planet is already full
So, I am your equity
and you are my social security
And the only savings there is
is what we can do for this world

And the truth is
I have an account here, at the dump
I'm accounting here, for the Earth
And we want an answer
past the stuff —

How much abundance is enough for you people?
What does it mean to be full-filled?
So hungry for justice
we spend mercy like money
I'm a reverse vending machine —
I give it all away
Subvert the curse of scarcity
so the whole world's transformed
to Robin Hood's hood
and our Age of Discovery
What's under that lid?
Cos I'm in recovery
Engage the cages
Free free trade
Bust open those closed dumpters
and then give it all away.

~ Eight ~

OIL SPILL

A hole in the bottom of the innocent sea
A hole in the bucket 5,000 feet deep
Through the blasting blowhole
the Gulf lies in it's casket
hemorrhaging

The damage we've let them do in pursuit
of human empowerment publishing
fresh definitions of sacrilege, our new mythology
The roots of this disaster are intensely personal
If we live at all
we live in collusion
Spectators
entertained in isolation
terrified and lied to
Everyday
life
is
a disaster

Oil woven like oxygen into every aspect of our daze

born into a world already wrapped in it's web
but there's another world
another web
Beyond the imperial cartels, the tanks of capitalism
the liars in charge of information will say
that coexistence is for extinct tribes, hippies and wild animals
Today, the Hopi's are saying it's their 7th prophesy
The Mayan calendar claims it too
The promised apocalypse — Al Quida, Satan —
Everyone wants a piece of this one
Jesus is coming back!

I say The Mother is rising up
Predictions comin' down like rain
All the paradoxes come home to roost
covered in oil
The Midas Touch turned inside out and backwards
What will our bank accounts, insurance plans, job security
mean
if the air is pestilence and the water affliction
And we, all alone on this earth, alive?
We loved oil, over all
and now we have it
over all
Killing and dying for this treasure
spilling and lying to ourselves and each other
All so we can package every bit of crap we buy
in plastic throw-away bags
and give em away for free by the billions every day
everyday, Everyday

The pursuit of our empowerment bursts
deep

A soundless roar under the bellowing sun
Our monster's a belief
that nature's a machine we can control
with our violent, sloppy ways
to feed our violent, sloppy lifestyles
She is alive
as we desecrate her, life giving
but wrathful as Kali
Our frankenstein monster making us mindful perhaps
of relations in other lands we gift with toxic garbage
military operations, nuclear power, global warming
Memory of Nature, dying at our blissed-out birkenstocks
We hear the drones passing over
It's over
We're all prisoners now
breathless
before her unleashed ferocity

And we watch live-feed of the earth's guts gushing
in real time
24 hours a day
Four hundred years after they declared the earth to be dead
she's coming alive
Chaos Theory unfolding before our eyes
Not a broken machine
but a butterfly wing
that bangs out a wind that trips the wire
of synchronized cascading failures
Even Boulder people
on their yoga mat path to enlightenment
risk
disturbance

In this dark empire that learns where foreign countries are
by bombing them
That learns about nature's circulatory systems
by poisoning them
We squat as settlers of America's 51st state
—state of Denial —
closer than Hawaii ever was
A river that hollows us out
leaks into every fissure
Pressurized, keeps us
mesmerized
so we gotta fight to feel the orphaned feelings
Feel the grief
— it's not paralyzing
it's just sadness
lets us know we care
So many asleep
and
so many targets
out there

Oh, Mother!
Super-size me for this task
Clone me to an army of healers
Months spent staring at the images
oil-poisoned pelicans, seals, turtles
Tasting blood on our sugared tongues
will we change now?
Hope so close to Denial
i don't trust it anymore
But hope has two beautiful daughters —
Anger
and

Courage
Will we change now, in love and in rage?
Can we stand in the fire
just burn
then Turn
for this earth that's our Mother
For this sin
of allowing the powerful
to speak for us?

Pray for awakening
Born again from this human error
this armor
not leaving this planet but re-entering it
A joyous reunion
Let go of controlling, separating
Close your eyes cos it's gonna hurt
Your cemented fortress peeling away bloody
like denial cauterized out of us
final fists unclenching
And we let it all go

Power devolving
bows to the revolution
volunteering in our hearts
Let go
and we'd let it all go
The illusion that money is wealth
so we'd know
that wealth is our potential to change
and we'd change
Rise to the task and we'd change
Just murmur forgiveness and change

Open our eyes
feel the wild lark of our wide open hearts
and we change
And we change state.

Deepwater Horizon Oil Spill,
April 2010

~ Nine ~

LABIDINAL MESSAGE

Libidinal, says the inner dictionary
        means
   all the instinctual energies that exist beyond this keyboard
  and my eyes
doing screen time
      Libidinal impulse:
             Im-pulse / I'm pulse/ I'm outta here
I hike out into the forest
       feeling that one thread of consciousness,
                 the running stitch

of my life
   flashing
  in and in and out
        I stand
     in a meadow bursting with seeds
    I am a meadow bursting with seeds
       while
mountains rise up all round me
   like mothers holding out blankets

The primary libidinous relationship is to the maternal body

A male genius called Freud said that.

Mother.
Other.
M/Other
To the male genius, women are Other
M/other Nature   (the ultimate Other)
spirals sequins through my pulses
chanting *Libidinal libidinal*

I walk into her song
The 10,000 things surround me.

Karl Marx said, *Humans are desiring machines producing libidinal materialism*
Oh fuck Freud
and fuck Marx too—
I've spent too many decades arguing with the Great Genius Man in my Head
The only question is—
How does life survive us?

The orange butterfly sinks her long tongue into the purple thistle head.
The one wind blows.

Post-Freudian Ecofeminists say
men **must** betray the feminine within themselves
The more different I am than mother, the safer I will be.
Father is the Master of Mother.
& Father is the Master of Matter.
And nothing female and free can survive it.

Libidinal,
from the same root as Labia,
the gateway —
We push through the hinge
escape the impoverished patriarchal heart

We're born through M/other, born to be Other, born to bear
this misogynistic world of male domination
where 'pussy' is the greatest insult a boy can call a boy
Where rape is the only possible response to lust
Where wilderness is scraped over, processed over,
barcoded over
where it is over
Dead at the feet of the genius men
& their ego-massaging women —
targets,
all
Where we are intermittent achievers at best
Hillary fiercely clashing
but absorbed into The Brotherhood of Suits.
Where women's work always involves mediating
between nature and culture.
Where it's all about food and dirt
and food and dirt
and exclusion and harassment and
We
are not particularly impressed
with self-interested speculation
exploitation
and technological advancement
for its (his) own sake

The butterfly fights the wind and her own big wings

to taste the sweetness a moment longer.

Is misogyny and separation from nature as simple and
as terrible as some Freudian negation of the mother?
Because infantile dependency to men is unspeakable,
as is the name Patriarchy —
try speaking it in mixed company
Patriarchy
It will upset
everybody.

Judaism projected a transcendent father god who is *not here*
Here are only machines, created by men
His magical uterus
"I'm no pussy"
M/other is only ever
and always
Pussy.

The Greeks split body and mind, subject and object.
Every monster in ancient Greece was female.
Greek misogyny revolting
against the feminine in all things
The Goddess of war emerges
fully armed from Zeus's head
She's no pussy.

— Science —
Detached manipulation
worshipping human mastery over a dead world
furthering man's emancipation from M/Other Nature.
— Religion —

teaching humans that we are separate
better than this butterfly, this sky
'cos
miserable cultures need a messiah
and an i-phone.

You can trash god, but I'm here to tell you
try trashing Science
and you've got a roomful of enemies
a world full of enemies.
Science — it's just separating and counting
man
and you're so good at it.
The tragedy of women and nature
counting
for nothing.

Europe's witch-hunts, paving the way for science and capitalism
biblical commandments, colonial terrors
commanding disenchanted nature
to Her death.
The age of Enlightenment meant
reductionism, dualism, straight lines,
meant *Progress*
The agonies of industrialization
and you know what—
FUCK ALGEBRA TOO!

Man created laboratory, competing with Labia
She creates life, but he creates death
This is patriarchy!
maximized - synthetic - commodity - production
value-added abstraction

that pierces the body of the one starved world
Her rhythms   whispering   *libido*
libido libido

Does any of this matter to the dew-beaded dragonfly
to the seeded rose hip?
I try to walk it off: e-motion, not e-stuckness.
Peace vibrates like bees in blossoms
like roots never still

The 10,000 things lean in
always and everything
like women
treading waters in our heated blood
In our repetitive domestic servicing
How invisibly we hold life and the world together.
Our unacknowledged labor, Mr. Marx, Mr. Freud, Mr. God
Our science   Our religion
unrewarded with a wage, ever and still
under every single institution
the emotional support, the material needs
so poorly understood
by male theorists
who walked straight out
of the only world
into a masculine fantasy of transcendent domination
but
left a hostage behind there--

Here: where being a Mother is the single greatest predictor of
poverty.
Here: where there is no language for us.

You know, even slaves had a language from
before
from when they were free
but not women
and surely

not Nature.

And all you'll see is how angry I am,
like
all we see is his utopian dream rising up all round us
call that *Life in the real world*
trained from birth to see dead roads paved with bullshit as
the real world
All landscapes are his
All language
and the contents of our minds too
Created by the force of his ideological machine
denying our libidinal foundation

That original cut from the mother's body numbed to the
ground
The shame of that first erotic link sealed off with asphalt
Nothing in Herself
like Women
laboring invisibly to free him up for self-actualization
Never a presence.
Never a voice.
A distant

throb
in the

pulses

The butterfly loses her grip on the blossom

Your science is changing the climate.
This dissociation in which we find ourselves
Now, finally
and very late,
a language to speak — *Environmental Crisis* —
a revelation
Now
Where the bodies of all species are under ineffable institutional-
ized attack

Here
At the end of progress
where the future hovers
between industrial disarmament
and
extermination

How
can some benevolent force
like a pair of Mama hands come down
and scoop us up
like an Internal Rapture
not leaving the planet
but reuniting it
Scoop us up
into
the sensual velvet enfoldment
the rapture of Mother Love

And it would hurt
your false identity burnt off, your armor peeling away
bloody
And then you'd be free.
We'd be free. ..

Life life life!
Oh Mama, keep holding out that blanket
Mama
Enfold us in your gargantuan safety
so we can let go
Like child soldiers and rescued lab animals
and rape survivors gotta learn to let go
Let that internal rapture
ripple a tsunami
the spectacle of science and violence cannot absorb

The mountain rises, grain upon grain and
disappears the same.

This circle
swaying like blossoms on stems
like waves on the beach
like the last tiger in a zoo cage
like this green supple mind
this red molten mind
While non-human Others quake and chase
soar, run and rain
we are one winged windy time bomb
The infinite wind chasing the shifting clouds
in the only sky
Panting hot beneath that boss of the sun
this grace of the moon
our cells and time
unwinding

While
the butterfly
vermillion-splashed

perfect against the blue
    is tossed again
        into This Wild World.

~ Ten ~

SACRIFICE, A STORY OF POWER

Falling through the eye of time
puny humans shout out to gods
tossing prayers like smoke
to the forces of the universe
till one eye opens in darkness

It has it's own plans but
we wake it, shake it, make deals with it
till power is ours, jumps through hoops on command
Why do they do it, these powers?
And what do they want in return?

Life inside a culture is Life, just the way things are
it breathes you inside it like the air
all that you believe is normalized
Humans crawl tenderly through the present on thin ice

The conqueror, history's author
tells us that Ancient Aztecs believed in human sacrifice
Calls them Heathens — appeasing with beating hearts
Calls them Barbarians — scaring even Conquistadores
Imagines lines of divine scapegoats

Says they fell like flakes
like flashes of fishes, turning direction as one up to heaven
levering the whole culture up higher towards god's good side

They tell us the Aztecs sacrificed to terrifying gods
Called one, *Enemy of Both Sides*
Called another, *We Who Are His Slaves*
If it's true that they called them with blood and fear
I say their relationship to that was clear
They didn't have mass media or science —
couldn't Google how it worked
— you just give 'em living human hearts
it makes the sun come up
The amazing invisiblilty of power
just the cost of breathing here.
We walk on thinning ice, sprinkling fairy dust
We're all slaves to god

In our time, we don't understand how electricity works
Oh, Technicians of the sacred
Xcel. Exxon. G.E.
You pray way out there over vast distances past
fiber-optic coal mines, industrial waste continents,
bandwidths to hell
One eye opens in darkness
Mountaintop removal. Fracking. Fukushima.
those haunted pipelines, those tortured wires
We flip the switch and
wall-to-wall powers grids inhale life
exhale fire
We worship,   from a distance,   on screens.

If we flipped that switch,

and blood started to pour down the temple walls
If we turned on this light and life crumpled to the ground
a mountaintop exploded, somebody strangles in a crib
a womin loses all her hair
Flip that switch and
nukes contaminate 10,000 generations
well
that's Progress.
We wouldn't call it
sacrifice
That word's too hot, like a beating heart
Give us keyboards, outlets, avoid at all cost
true contact with the world
We learn to call *the real world* our jobs
We bend science backwards to avoid sacrificing anything
We don't call it murder — just the way things are

They numb us with data
swaddle us in darkness
We beg the gods for blindfolds just keep the lights on
Our minds, colonized as banana plantations
while we feed the world to our machines

It's a story, it's a prayer for power
It's Progress — what they say you can't stop
It's Progress — which could be called *Escalation*
It's not a primitive myth, it's Science, it's our god
You press this button, the Power comes on

Enemy of Both Sides. We Who Are His Slaves
We flip that switch, blood starts flowing rivers
no one here is running for their lives or screaming in the streets
Sludge fills rivers, the air and oceans toxify

radiation is a verb
Science doesn't say
We are all slaves of god who created the world for humans to dominate
Science just acts like it

Aztec people knew it took tremendous sacrifice
to keep gods happy
What do we know?
We flip that switch. Something happens
We don't know what it wants
or why or how
We just join the great apocalypse
a traffic jam on thinning ice
Whaddaya gonna do?
Organize a resistance movement against gods?
Do you believe everything the conquerors say—
or are you ready to blockade with our bodies
the blood soaked altars
of those temples?

~ Eleven ~

WATER PROTECTORS

The Missouri pours the longest river in America
It flows into the Mississippi
near Fergusen, birthplace of Black Lives Matter
Flows past old southern plantations
fields and graves and lynching trees
It flows past New Orleans where
a hurricane response created a racist catastrophe
that washed a city clean of poor people
Flows into the Atlantic Ocean
where five centuries ago, slave-stealing ships
followed smoke of burning witches
paving the road for empire —
Christianity/Science/Capitalism
— colonial schism forever erasing pagan cultures
Histories flow together like rivers
like pipelines
Victors forget how they get their spoils
but the de-spoiled remember
Water remembers

By the Cannonball River
banners pop in the wild winds

Black Snake Kills
No DAPL!
Navajo social media fairy said
through her wind-whipped hair
"Prayer is simple —
You say *Help me.*
You say *Thank you.*"
And off she blew to the front lines
of this most recent Dakota showdown

Before there was Facebook
Deep-Time people sent out drum stories
Ancestors of these same horses whinnied
prancing under an older sky
where children ran free and full
life unrolling like a peaceful river
till the invaders shot them all down
Time and the river flow on

Home, now
writing poems in a room full of cables
nourished by satellites, pipelines and snakes
but haunted by history
Rushing whitewater beams from Facebook Hill
where they're indigenizing media with digital smoke signals
Live feeds story-tell prophesies —
black snake is devouring the world
Capitalism's rivers choking on pipelines
The seven generations circle a fresh confluence
chant and drum: the whole world is watching
It's simple, she said
Help me.
Histories flow together

Thank you.

Elders sit in cheap folding chairs
while warriors gallop the endless body of wind
flaming arrows sending pixels across their land
The raised fists/ fires/ feathers/ drums,
the tanks/ tipis / teargas/ babies/
the calm, beautiful horses
all together facing down armies of the conqueror
Mni Wiconi they say
Water is life
Ceremony broadcast over a bandwidth of wind and eagles
My bones the rattle
my heart the drum
Pierced like a Sundancer with visions
earth and water, fire and air
Great Mystery of living rivers/ forests/ animals
that fierce rudder, closing distances
My voice and arms raised with theirs
We say *Help me.*
We say Thank you
Prayer
a gossamer net
in love with the future
tossed over all there is

~ Twelve ~

PALIMPSEST

"As many of you know, Ruby Montoya and I have engaged for the past year in various forms of what we believe to be peaceful resistance against the Dakota Access pipeline. In July, 2017, Ruby and I claimed responsibility for having undergone an 8-month-long property destruction campaign against DAPL infrastructure in an effort to halt construction." (Jess Reznicek)

Written on the Wo-man-U-script of their bodies
in disappearing ink
their story
lingers, fades
And you won't have heard of them
these women
because empire covers sabotage with
fresh DowJones headlines of enrichment
but
spiral down like a seed
under the head- lines, the dead-lines
the pipe-lines
read between beneath these lines
scratch the surface and you can see it
An interspecies howl
under papyrus, vellum, parchment

separate the layers to find what's preserved there
Palimpsest —
immutable underlay of truth

On election day
they torched 6 massive destruction machines
burnt em to the suffering ground
Two girls taught themselves to destroy empty pipeline valves
and Acted
their arson inspiring others to Act, boldly
Cut off the supply lines
Go deeper

Today I walk with sticks
four-legged
to ease the pain in me
and beneath this foggy body
feel the sharp animal
of another body
as real as this one
Under this pain, a well body
as underneath this mined-blasted-poisoned earth
is another
waiting in her power
for geology and consciousness to rise
and shake it all off
— Palimpsest

Their names ring through my skull
disappearing beneath darkness
like pipelines
like tales of sabotage against the machine
Jess and Ruby

deconstructive tools of alternate iterations
Like the holy lands buried beneath churches
Like witches
created by the land to defend the land
tortured, burned, and
I don't know if they'd call themselves *witches*
yet
Under the Tar Sands
Under the Mississippi River
Under the pipelines, beneath prophesy
I write their names
in crystal green
in azure
in malachite
in armed words guarded by living fires
Protectors

The angle of light is changing
layers separating
The earth has turned enough to tell
turned to burn
tell it yelling
buried tales that must be told
generations of resistance
overlaid with the official story
Encrypted, it's all there
Subjugated populations rise up
sheer as the Great Divide
Subalterns tossing up portals
like vellum, like papyrus
that's been scraped, over-written
and buried in darkness--
Genesis is literal: *let there be light!*

As autumn looms over exhausted summer
surrounded by crumpled flowers
or whispers of interlocking dependencies
we learn who we are
and the moral of the story
or
this is where the tale ends
stuttering a language of longing
Drown in the paradox
strobing
love and rage, love and rage
love
and
rage
A song to guide me
into this one power
As we accelerate
into a silver skyworld
desperate as wolves
inside algorhythmic steel traps

Oh, disciplined anarchists of the underground
we chew off our feet in resistance
we unearth the impermanent pavement
to reveal our secret manifesto
We delay
disrupt industrial anguish and false necessities
the denial they escort us thru daily
We're the unfinished animal
running from all the dazzling forecasts
Running together like thieves in the night
shaking off the might of trauma

the dust, like wild animals do
Buried underlings ready to rise up
scraping through lies with a fork and a knife
devour the shallow surface
Bared teeth
crouching under economic electronic structures
awakened to the pour of waterfall lies
to be their undoing

Servants of earth and all her calderas
carving every satellite out of the skies
with your courage
Leading the people out of the darkness
So many of us
sensing the remedy
from our barely felt tails
to where the forest grows up and over us
Beyond that insatiable desire for refinement
where we remember all of it
engathered we spark
in your name
we flame
we engulf
we explode
we knock em
alive!

~ Thirteen ~

SUSPICIOUS BEHAVIOR

Please report any suspicious behavior.
The warning repeats robotic as Satan's heartbeat
I approach concourse B
swimming through another recording
music piped into airy arc of skybridge
disembodied as that warning
surreal as this landscape
Indians' recorded chanting
flutes and drums swirl, voices keen
Savage irony of Native American exploitation continues
Could it be an aural trojan horse?
Maybe warriors will leap into our pink heads
through our silver ears and conquer us now?
Re-take this land, starting with DIA skybridge?
(i'd never report that to you bastards)

Dark sudden grip of Homeland Security.
The lines. The paramilitary uniforms. The recorded warnings.
It's like a freshly conquered nation here.
Within the fascist shadow, i remove
coat, scarf, belt, shoes, computer

many plastic bins hold my life sliding away
stripped down in an endless lineup
faith-based commuting
We watch helpless
as belongings disappear
through the evil conveyor belt of radiation
big brother thinks he can see inside my heart
no fucking way, or he'd never let me fly

"Miss!" Some guy is calling, "Miss!"
I look around and there, inside a glass box
like a giant Barbie on display
a middle aged white dude
shoeless and beltless,legs spread
taps the transparent wall to get my attention
"I think my cell phone's in with your shoes."
Behind him, uniformed goons
are running wands over another freedom loving body
"Miss..."
He speaks to me as if nothing — him in the box, me in my socks
the radioactive wanding, or his words — are strange
I check — "Nope. Not with my shoes."
I silently wish him courage and move on towards the skybridge
the dematerialized chanting voices
Indian spirits hover, amazed
What degradation won't these fools put up with
in the name of *safety*?
They must be cracking up, wherever they are now
What terrible humiliations won't we grow used to
like this ridiculous theater can keep us safe
from millennia of karma
coming down like poison-tipped arrows
Everywhere around me people are re-lacing their shoes

putting their shit back together, comforting their children
waiting in wheelchairs, being scoped and wanded
A display of adaptation — our most dangerous superpower

Under the video "The Extreme Ice Survey", I stop
my habit to pay homage to this nightmare unraveling
No one ever watches this show, it seems, but me,
and I watch everytime
breathing my mortal breath to this insensate pixelated loop
the glaciers of Antarctica, time lapsing, collapsing
No way to adapt to this
but we do
On the screen, acres of glaciers collapse
travelers pass with eyes averted
as they do with the homeless on every corner.
Don't look. Your attention can make it real
the threat level is orange

I stand there
shut my eyes
sink into my root
shift weight into the left leg
Tai chi: a counterbalance
Distant glaciers surrender in unreal time to the urgent music
Gateway of wrists, shoulders, elbows open
Beside the action screen, a mural of Antarctic ice fields
Relax the elbows. Shift weight. Turn.
At the lowest left hand corner,
a tiny human figure in an orange anorak
faces the vastness
like science
I hold the world
Like a human

Step out
The music flows all round me
Relax, I say inside, *relax*
I face the ruined fields of ice, step
follow my hips swinging slowly to the corner
face airplanes taking off and landing out the wall-tall window
Nobody stops. Nobody slows. No one dares
to watch me trace
this ancient pattern of gratitude
here before the shredding modern world

The airplanes zoom off with the speed of glacial collapse
time lapse, the madness of motion
Relax
grasp the sparrow's tail
Music tumbles as ice tumbles
urgent as planes zooming off, as unseen departure time nears
a barely contained panic oozing in the air
I slow it all down
The melting poles, the latte-inhaling people,
the jets blasting off and landing
lift
turn
single-whip
The terror alert has been raised to Orange
but the ice is clean as prophesy
this story unfolding, our only future
— our response, air travel —
The sign beside the streaming video images says
We believe that global warming is a non-partisan issue
How the fuck did they get to put this vdo display here,
facing runways— did they win an Irony Grant?
win in a tie

with the chanting tribes hovering over the sky bridge?
White crane spreads her wings
brush knee
shift weight
push
Stand in the middle like this
invisible, like they are —
the convulsing ice, the native spirits, the endless war, the irony
push
turn
I'm standing inside a bubble of freaky otherness
it's the only thing bold enough to survive here
moving on, sideways through the world
past cameras and badges
through incessant uniforms & warnings

Please report any suspicious behavior
I'm looking for a public phone, a public clock —
how suspicious is a human body lacking a cell phone these days?
My phone book is an actual phone book
I have to ask strangers the time
—*have to talk to strangers*—
stand fearless in my skin without a screen to shield me
Make eye contact
here, in this public space
absent of public clocks and public phones

The threat level has been raised to orange.
Fucking liars— it's been orange for 9 years
Suspicious means you don't blend. I don't blend
also, I'm invisible, and how suspicious is that?
Another oxymoron to toss on the irony pile
looming taller as glaciers shrink to puddles

looming above the disgrace
race relations & a melting planet
& the guy in the box
& the lines of passengers who live inside
unquestioned security
as giant billboard images of happy shiny people bear witness
to all the stressed out, miserable crowds rushing past
As the Dow Jones flows past on tickertape
how do we just keep going forward?
This culture is a blender
engines of denial
cruelty of privilege
worship of ignorance
whirs us all into brutally indifferent blades
and if you don't grab hard
hold fast to the ragged edge of the farthest wall
you'll be shredded by the jagged teeth
— homogenized

I'm holding fast
the roar is all there is
It substitutes for our screams
If only we could run all our machines on cognitive dissonance
cos that shit'll never run out
our hearts stilled to obedience
waving our flags with our shoes in our hands
Please report any suspicious behavior
i really don't know
where the fuck
to begin

~ Fourteen ~

HYSTERECTOMY

Part One

Removing my lady bits
feels
extreme as a mission to Mars
abstract as Mama dissolving in her coffin
Bulls-eyed between belly button and vulva
anonymous technicians take digital coordinates
Power source or just a lost
& vacant space
waiting for cancer to come
and unpack his dark blue bags?

Here, at the hot spring
under the morning trees
I blast off towards his inexorable hands
fit to drive robot fingers
to cut the bits fitted
inside me
out.
Inside me: men's eyes and robots
cameras, mirrors, saw-blades, a bag....

how will it all fit
inside 4 tiny slits
down there?
Sun in the green branches
whispers with me:
fare thee well to the organ of life
the mystery dissipates
aging like yesterday's sliced peaches
flesh marbled with the effort of life losing vigor
seeds dessicated and over it
—this bowl stares me down.

Hormone means Messenger.
Who will be my messenger now?
Just this chemical squirt from Walgreens?
I've had enough messages
ya know, it's late and
the machine's full
and
i'm droppin' out
of evolution's party so
I guess I'll take it from here.

Here
where
messengers on tiny bikes
speed to and from the brain
carryin' mystery substances
down the steep hill of spine
that central switchboard smokin'
telegraphing taps and spaces
traces of someone
whisperin' into the ear of this world

somehow connected to
hopeful grandmother ancestors
knitting little cervical caps
to fit a blooming uterus
and winter coming on.

Will the loyal messengers abandon their bikes now?
Just a flesh garage full of twisted wheels
rusting pedals and gears
and no further communication?
Only an empty room
uninhabitable, but safe
while some receptors wait
for the missives that will never come
wait
through this sunset time
taps blowing softly across the old pink sky—

Just the cosmic letdown of leisure,
like when they say *her milk's come down*
but this is my Life
come down
to this:
a cenote
completely self-contained
and leading nowhere.

Oh, Lady Bits
unseen wilderness of
unthinkable shapes in fantasy shades--
hot pink, deep purple
blinking bruised and heavenly blue
pulsing, pumping— oceanic

as a desert.
Farewell
to all that tender tissue
and toehold
launchpad and sill
patient but poised
waiting mindlessly
through convulsive replications
and preparations
the mechanics of a bowling lane
a lifetime of pins
knocked down and set back up
tirelessly
through strikes and spares
the ball sent back
thanks to
mysterious subterranean tubes
over
and over
infrastructure --
we don't like to think about it.
On and on, like a pep-squad
like a volleyball team
running laps round a frozen lake
arms raised, indefatigable
all that work! All these years!
And so, nostalgia
is the least I can offer
gratitude for an unwanted miracle.

(Maybe it'll be a girl robot, or a womyn's volleyball team
    spiking, diving, passing balls and blades)

I track coordinates
walk the long lines of rigor
with clipboard and checklist
wanting poetry like wings to lift me out
of this distant mystery
this body cavity
echoing bowling alley/ cenote/ bike garage/
this stadium of pink clad gladiators
where women do push-ups on chair-backs
and jog round the morning track
Here, this
airy profusion of thoughts
is a silver-spun windmilling mind
where I hide
from fire-red saws
the waiting O.R.

I write leaning on my abdomen
trying not to think of 4 deep punctures
that'll enter my gut like swords and
after the knife-fight
which I will win
with my army of pink girl-robots
volleyball champions
and female bike-messengers
there will be peace
and space

Part Two

Oh, tender Pussy
hollowed out sacred chalice

holy crimson witness
to being female in this world
The wise wound that watches
who howls in holy hunger
and danger
waiting for it
Attractor of atrocities
target of patriarchy
Superpower —
It was time.

To the door that was open
and the door that is closed
I bow.
To the one abortion that wrecked me for years.
To the dear deified and despised lady parts.

Farewell to the rapes, to being a victim.
Farewell to hearing that I wanted it
To all the dicks, real and imagined
for all that misplaced fear of strangers—
To the rape anxieties gifted me
by my grandfather and my friends' fathers
my father's friends and the man I babysat for
and the date rapes, a surprise every time
and the incest fading now, but not ever, not really
To every finger, breath and thought that was shoved into me
To all the shrapnel that's burrowed inside
to simply vanish there
trapped deep within
that I calcified
in my wisdom
to bone

Farewell
Yahweh and Adam, Abel and Caine
All y'all and your damned sons
lining up and taking turns
with me and my sisters
acting like it was nothing
like we all forgot, and went on
so sure of ourselves, *never*
Only the stumble, the traumas tumbled
to smooth stones
to fossils of bone
till we act as if they didn't
because we wouldn't....
As if all that shredded/embedded trauma
were a bad dream, a bad move
and it was
and it is.

Carted off now as medical waste
turned to stone
like memories
turned to bone
like some funky pearl
in a luminous shell.
Only this grit, this gate
this thing called rape
legitimized by them
swallowed by us
We
who never had power in their world
—their desire is NOT our power! —
Women

so strong
we can carry all these acts
inside this tiny pubic bermuda triangle
to our graves and beyond
to our daughters' graves and beyond
women ribboning our lives
like an arrow through
Hey girl, why don't you smile?
Why don't you like me?
Why don't you act
like you're enjoying it?
pretty ribbons make shitty shields
and it will all be over
eventually.

Farewell to the Red Energy
to the hopeful stubborn eggs that just kept coming
even tho they weren't gonna to meet anyone
No rookery, no bud
a different fertility
as it ever was in this dyke body
Womb as sense organ
enfolding all lunar possibilities
for a new myth birthing
here
Just a ruby-jeweled space
beyond rivers of desire, surrender, receptivity
With what will I replace that space?
Only give me power to express
how fertile I am, still
with myself
I fill me in with ME
and more

sacred coloring book
spreading in time
as I relinquish
and replenish
the holy pearl
of my only mission
to full
again.

Summer 2015

~ Fifteen ~

LIKE-LANGUAGE

Language is a weapon of power
used to destroy the expressive abilities of the powerless
by destroying their sense of reality. (Andrea Dworkin)

I am the guard at lingo's gate
i point my only weapon— poetry —
at humanity's conquerors
and their data-drenched gadgetry
Fight 'em bare-handed
whistle-slick and silver-tongued
with a pen

In every human landscape
crowds stream past
Little white wires snaking from pockets to ears
looking like their heads are being transfused
and they are
these descendants of Alien Nation
receiving commands from the Mother Ship
Texting, chatting, shopping, dating
absorbing
everything
and nothing

They call instead of visit cos it's faster
They text instead of call, cos it's faster
They date on line
speed date and speed marry
and speed divorce each other
and the land

Like talk —
language
dumbed
d
o
w
n
degraded and
so clearly a cry for help
A try to connect to another mind
to bridge alienation
And I was like and she was like and it was like.... right?

Dig it —
— *LIKE*
It's a metaphor
this is like that
an exchange of energy that connects the world
Omigod! No way! I mean...
Right? *Right?*
only.....
can we even follow each other out on this crazy slim limb
thinnest subjectivity of self adrift
in unmapped chaos-enslaved journeys?
Do you know what I mean?
Communion. The beloved community.

Sanga. Hold me closer.

It's empty and its hungry
It's a baby crying out for mommy
Its meaning slid away and sliding faster
It's language that reflects the master plan
the hidden disaster
Adorable and pathetic like a motherless kitten
like language banging around in internal space
never written
And somewhere out there on Planet Irony it's really beautiful
'cos language is relational, indicational
but, like
we got no operating instructions for humans
becoming cyborgs
So
we chase on fractured feet
across dissolving space
in a race
to be held
in that common
embrace

We're one sightless eyeball
like a lens covered by a sock pulled down over it
like we're blinded when seeing's the only thing that'll save us
this post post modern world's just like erasing us
a vast impurity of isolation
the perfect vernacular for our times
outspoken or inspoken
affliction fluent glossolalia
Mangled, scattered, gaseous and perfectly passive
Like the wars, like advertising

like corporations
enshrined with human rights
like civilization's corruption of community
it's like the total destruction of unity
Like cell phones, ring tones,
the machine voice that answers every phone
like I phones, I pads, I pods, I feelings
It's like the dream of living closer and closer to our machines —
Do you know?
Do you know what I mean?

We learn this life sideways
teachin' by reachin'
mind to mind and mindless habitual
Its like a ritual who's priestesses have all died
Like the lies of repartee leading us into the fog
mouths first
sounding this incoherent
No way to break out of this breakdown
its like the brakes are on us now
Lazy and flimsy idiot-dialect
mirrors our inability
to think about anything critically
Born again into this silicon reality
I say we were born right the first time
then they got a hold of our minds
turned us all into mimes
We got our brains juiced
now we play charades just to get through
It's all about control
a response to being silvered-over in abstraction's arms
the very language of thought dis-arming us
It's like *We give up!*

Bound to a sneaky squeak of system
repeating the status quo's styrofoam dictum
affliction diction
Where machines are the only ones
precise and efficient
While we sit in shadows encircled by lies
circumscribed
our degenerate confusion a rope tied tight
whooping it up in the firelight
no illumination or insight
The only light that emanates
is from our screens
while evolutionary brains sit
bound and gagged in darkness
absorbing thrills
and mumbling bullshit

Oh, wake me when my people have promise again!

And this morning,
my friend said to me
Yeah, so I was like, you know, whatever.
That is like a direct quote
Whatever
like
I don't have a preference
Like, paper or plastic? Whatever.
And in a way it's heroic
like I'm not falling for this fake & fucked up choice
like my voice makes a fuckin' dent in any of it, motherfucker
why'd you even ask me?
Or, like I don't have a strong enough mind

to not buckle under a shitty choice
Or, like I'm too busy to be bothered caring
like I'm so cool I can be this lazy
or, I don't believe I'm important enough
smart enough to get to choose
And you're so right
And you're so following orders

And then
there's the airy spokesperson
for the party of massive vague optimistic stupidity who says
It's all good.
Says, smiling at you
No worries.
Cowardly bastard!
Blind, lying, denying fool--
I hate that guy
It is not all good
Pull that sock off your head, dummy!
These people are hypnotized
and they're trying to hypnotize *you*
Run away from them
Confront them
Shake em till they wake up
or break apart into useful pieces
so we can start again

We've become machine components
upgrading ceaselessly
sounding more like 30 second infomercials
than fine minds
now that humans advertise themselves
in accordance with the market

Corporations concoct communities, but
life is more complicated
crowded
and critical

You're so, like, crazy.

Like, like yeah? Like I'm a nearly perfect facsimile of crazy
but not actually crazy?
Stop it!"
Like stop it or really stop it?

Why are we not running in the streets and screaming?
We would do that if a stranger started shooting in
a midnight Batman movie,
a high school, a mall, a Mosque, a McDonalds
or another like random attack
This is so much worse than that!
This. Is. So. Much. Worse.
Right?
i mean......you know
We got Stupid for President
are at war with a noun
it's like, you know.....
do you know what I mean?

~ Sixteen ~

UNDER THE PRAYER SHAWL

all day making out
with the phenomenal world
one bird
bowing before nature
one scholar
endlessly reading
flat & busy pages
— i wish i believed in god —
any god
in the voice moving like a chord
over the land
heavy with answers
avatars of vishnu
woodland fauns and corn spirits
teach me
lakshmi, pan, artemis
tutelar holy dogs. jupiter.......
enormous shadows of divinity
stalking us
the word made flesh, made mine
mana. wakan. obeah
persephone, kali, morgana, all y'all

the madonna and all her vampires in heaven
'o father of lies — embed me above your perverted bed
zion, avalon, nirvana
my mother's house
chaos: the sacred center
i levitate into space

i drop the masks
cover my face
a simple gesture
peek-a-boo
thumbs to my cheekbones, fingers to my brow
hands tent my breath, eyes shielded
i calm my explosive frontal lobe

breathe
and
the walls shatter
the books are glitter raining down
words fly
into the blue black air
detonated
as i am

i pray
as my Mother prayed
as her Mother prayed
hung like Inanna
for the sins of our power
sepia faded lives of ancestors
ribbon like rivers of rain
across continents and centuries
inherited bandwidth

continuous
accompanies me
in that perennially dripping
forest of do-overs
silent thunder calls me home
far beyond where winds have blown
waking into realms unknown
where the world is
green, red
and endless

zooming over illumined thresholds
back to the magical caves
ancient painted temple walls
— not god, but belonging —
the sacred mammalian longing to Be with your kind
the clapping, the swaying
the familiar-foreign language flickering
on the threshold of my 6th decade
separate at last from mama's body
like that astronaut treading black space
air hose dangling
tumbling like that for years
i say i've been making up a religion
to fit **my** life and **this** world
i say it's empowering
and lonely as hell

next day
taps blowing softly
across the old pink sky
i return to shul
inside a knowing that

i'm forgiven by angels
mingle with the fasting masses
find a laddered rack of prayer shawls
blue on white
find behind language
the serene departure of the veil
the recessed retreat
disappearing
in full view of everyone
into my hearts' garden
the untouchable solitude
inscrutable silence
poof....

you cover your face
sway and disappear
into the colors of your own exhale
just surrender
is this where mama went
when she left me
and the world?

beneath the prayer shawl
an inner sanctum
where
you stand like a pillar
a holy ashera tree
the weight of the fabric sinks my roots
down
how it curves over me
folds me in like batter
how i flow
an upside down waterfall

how i am pushed deeper
backwards through space
spun
through rivers of stars
beyond exalted thought
just
one distinct jewel in a string of beads
wed to a myth
one shard of the pot
someone who's never done this before
someone who's done this forever
the blue blur of forever
how many shards of desire
years of beads spent swooning
strung
out
wheeling like spray in the milky way
holy breast milk
feeding all the lonely astronauts
this linkage
leading like lava
one gesture, one prop
  peek-a-boo
archetypes weep from their hiding places

next morning i sit in sunshine
face the grave up the mountain
something high
deep
and fresh-ancient circles the land
lifting me
to the Shekhinah
here

a desert sprouting green promises
un-scrolling
across the open skies of me
my fingers all over it
on the inside
the one sky exhales one bird
disappearing
& arriving
again........again

~ Seventeen ~

LOVE POEM TO MY BODY

Now
when the most repeated phrase of my life has become
I need to sit down.
Now
when the tug of gravity threatens to bury me under rubble
of my own collapsing bones
Now
when I walk into a room and scan for a comfortable chair
like i used to scan for a beautiful woman
Now, I am gathering the love I have
for you
Old Thing

Old thing, who has carried me far
Old thing, who will never leave me
Loyal old dog, losing muscle mass like fur
shedding bone density and expectations
I do not anticipate depth of rigor
will not challenge you to do more than feels good
Feeling good: what was that about?
Every day there's pain

some days better than others and yet
I worship you--
You, who look so much better than I feel
You, who show up at parties and in circles
at the head of classrooms
and on stage dressed in costumes
so sexy, so full of life force energy
And show up in Xrays
and MRI's in staggering debilitation
I love you.

Old thing, still kickin it
even when I can no longer cross my legs
put on shoes and socks
dance at all or stand for long or walk very far
What it's like
to measure distance with my eyes
and decline every subversive incline
This dissent against the pull and drag
plowing through thickened mediums of air
now it's uphill all the way
What's it like to rest in daylight
at the window
like an abandoned dog
to feel invalid-dated in human company?

Now, I gotta reach deep
as strangers will reach deep
while I'm intubated with anesthesia
dreaming, while they saw off my femur
dislocate my leg from my torso
and make titanium live here for the rest of this journey
Hip hip hooray, y'all

I've never lost any part of me before
that was physical
I've lost my mind and my heart
splintered attention like a block of wood in winter
spent my focus
and splayed my mind over the smoker
but this body has remained intact
except for 2 teeth

Oh body, Old Thing
This is us in extremis
As the forest grows taller outside the window
& stillness becomes the only way to be out of pain
as we learn to say No more
as our wild winds wrap the planet in endless frenzy
This mind climbs the ladder of spine
snaking like a caduceus dreaming of wellness
I dream of wellness
now

And love is the least I can do
to pay you back for all the beauty
all the joys of this long trip
exhausted by the journey
unraveling mind-first
load-bearing joints to follow
watching the wild birds fly
fills me with anticipation
for the next lifting surprise
step to the edge and rise
that's what I'm holding this morning
and visions of my alter-ego

sexy on that stage
before the loving crowd last night
crowds out the pain of today
as I gird my tired loins
to do it all over again
the night before
the knife bite
tomorrow

~ Eighteen ~

THE FALL

Today, the market's falling
autumn leaves are falling
instructions for uprising coming down with falling leaves
and the waiting's almost done.
The second industrial revolution is the one *against* industry
freeing us from the wars, the toxins, the mastery
Free us like trees into sharing, resting
and merciful silence

Seeds: prepare yourselves for yourselves
Friends: prepare yourselves
like autumn rattles falling
walk out into the glittering groves in silence
Once the standard was gold, now we're told trust in god
but I swear allegiance to this earth
Back to the ground
found in the land of the lost
still counting the cost
the endlessness of life finding her way
to the beat of every rhythm this culture's destroyed
keeps me counting

down

Trust in bags of beans and rice
gardens and gallons of olive oil
Trust in rain, community, in gravity, self sufficiency
we were always each others' social security
Celebrate when the blue wind shakes her tambourine and
leaves sail down
the aroma of decay blessing life with insurrection
Trust the direction of down
Sink into the ground, exhausted
as aspens shimmy out of their tender underwear
and leaves drop like silken panties to the forest floor
Crown the homeless, the crazies, and all cleaning ladies
and drop down, fall down, crash down
like the walls of Wall Street
like the tanks of free trade

They made this land an aircraft carrier, an armed satellite
but the messenger from the barricades came
reading singed strips of light
Beware the lies: that's the only rule now
Sit. Take your shoes off. Breathe
Just step aside, crumble into compost,
leaf on
fall ....
away from bulldozers and alarm clocks
gas pumps and sharp objects of danger
Fall.

Prepare to enter the forest
ask forgiveness
Season of atonement when we'll eat the seeds of roses

as the earth empties her silence into things of noise
Wonder is the question that asks us now
our unfinished animal selves
laughing like grass in parking lot cracks
Deathless, I add my breath to your breath
and breathed by life
we fall again into
the Great Mothering Soul

Fall into this world again
Her dark ecstatic galaxies craving form
the language of longing fruiting
inside our gorgeous imaginations
our pockets full of seeds
our sacks of rice and beans
and the naked truth of winter
circling closer

~ Nineteen ~

SIRI!

All hail Siri!
GPS-- Girl Positioning System
How I long to gaze into your metallic eyes
In a landscape of trance, you mesmerize
Michigan blueberry farms, gun stores
Amerikkkan flags and You
mineral-mined oversoul of the merge and flow
I love it when you tell me what to do!

Way down here
in your unfathomable dark, I came alive
Found my way into the light of another world
SIRI!
I forget the direction of the blood traveling the roads of my veins
But *you* know
Your silver zeppelin consciousness floats
lunar,   female
through outermost space
engorged on our aimless desires
You —cosmic constant of relative continuum
You — Post Modern Cyber Goddess of Wisdom
You lead me on like Circe

wearing MonaLisa's smile
You watchin' over me like Mary
You —
burnin' way out there like Joan of Arc
        in the dark

Your metallic dreams flash on alabaster screens
above forests, beaches, garbage dumps of great cities
Knowing every crease and fold, street and road
and even parking lots where we lose
our ways and our souls
Racing thru the onrush of industry & monoculture
in a trackless unity of trade, warfare and technics
— wheels carry us through
never losing contact with You

You murmur our technological origin story
in hot, binary-sequence breath
straight into my receptive heart
I summon you and
you ohm-boom down from 12,000 miles up
drop anchor in my frontal lobe,
check your algo-rhythmic hair in mirrored RV windows
O, SIRI —you look as good as you sound, girl
Rubbing the scan of land
making the most outrageous suggestions!
I bow down
my body the pendulum you muscle test
against your own vast memory
Timestamp and measure me
map me like that
Oh honey, surveil me!

Clouds, rivers, velocity groovin'
warm carseat movin' under vibrations of your voice
choice-less as the ores that made you
'O, Unity of All Sentient Humans
tell me what to do!
Where am I right now
against the When of you?

I surrender.

Giant machines in space
link up
through total information awareness
connect to my speck of light
way the fuck down here
pulling stoned wheelies of confusion
on unlit back roads
Here I am!
One frustrated tiny blue dot
on a map
on a borrowed phone screen
on a road
on a planet
of ten million roads
.... special like that ....

Here in the fast lane, in a semi-sandwich
finding my gyropilot overdrive
finding that...What!? —
Illinois has Indiana shoved in there between it and Michigan —
No shit!
What mortal could predict these mysteries?

Oh, Quantum-Isis, great accomplice
fan me back to the land of the living
with your tungsten wingspan
your sacred weightless orbit of military surveillance
And, here's something, kids
SIRI changes gender at will!
She/ He/ They
is fucking revolutionary like that!
Surely
the Patriarchy cannot survive Her !
..... They..... Them......damn.

You say *"Check it out, Lin"*
You say *"OK, Lin, here's what I've got"*
Oh Siri!
How I long to know what it is that you've got
beneath that pixelated bustier
under those liquid-fuel panties —
Details, i want details!
No, that's auto detailing
No, that's Denny's, babe
Say MY name in your
calm yet-slightly-breathless femme voice––
Say it!

If only this were MY smartphone
You would speak My name
into the silver void of my own head.
I would tell you to call me
Queen of Your Over-Flowing Crystal Pussy
and you would —
Such devotion to duty!
O info-dedicated beauty —

Cosmic conductor waves her baton
interstellar cloud-bright wand
above the fresh bloodstained interstates
Extend my fickle reach
straddle and drive me
hot shepherd me to my target
Hook me up, baby!

Writhing in roving geo-synchronous anticipation
I wanna suck on your satellite nipples
lick your titanium clit
scissor your pole-star thrusters
& gaze into yr GPS eyes
Entranced by landscapes of melting tar
and endless fucking highway construction
your rocket-deployed heart searches
pulsing above the nation
— in the eyes of birches
the curve of yield signs
dendrites of infants &
the wild skid-marks of the passionate highway—

Entrained to your stupendous space walk
I oscillate across undulating terrain
an oriented blue dot
piloted by your fly-by probes
your colossal projections surround me
we all know better
and yet,
I reject the dominant paranoia!

You *are* our monstrous future enemy assassin,
true —

but You find me a Denny's in the middle
— a sizzle in that griddle
oh, something in the middle to live for after all!
and You knew that
You know everything!
"Watch out for that semi truck, Lin!"
I'm not Lin, dammit!
SIRI says,
"Breathe Lin."

And you steer me to mooring, and i miss you already
interconnected
and deathless
embedded
in
breathtaking cascades of mining & labor
fatal crashes and fundamentalisms
high-tech servers, traffic detours
serial killers, military targets
I surrender to You
Mystic Gadgetron
because here we are
surrounded by meth labs in a landscape of dreams
all watched over
by dormant killing machines
of such
self-reflective
grace.

~ Twenty ~

CHANGING THE STORY

Democracy and Capitalism are antagonistic
and this is important as we all go autistic
trading cleverness for wisdom-- narrowed in and narcissistic
All that we call the GNP
is nothing but the sum of our atrocities
recording the planet's dismemberment
and the stock market's where we bet on death

Wall Street was built as a market for slaves, and still
billions are made to slave in poverty
'cos that's the story of Imperial Security
Millions of species melting like snowflakes
while we stand numb as sheep in pens
All creation wasted for the profits of a few rich men
and they decide value and how we spend

Packaging that lasts 300 years
to wrap what it takes 3 minutes to eat
We drive armored tanks to the PTA meeting
use nuclear power plants to toast our bread
We need to change the empire story

because money is dead

Humans live by stories
The king is in his counting house
and all of patriarchy's been one single story
broadcast like a bullet from a gun
Shouting: defend with your lives the counting houses of the king!
Yelling: War and Profit! Fear and Greed!
Private property is sacred
riches are for the few
Disobedience is a sin
and obedience a virtue
And it's that *story*
not armies or politics
that's the empires' greatest power
But now is the hour
to change the story

Cos we're the best-dressed most overfed slaves in history
and it's the constant repetition of this story
convinces us we're free
But now there's a tear in the story
What they call crisis is a chance for choice
To know ourselves as just one voice
in a gorgeous chorus of life on earth
We're the unfinished animal
that's our wealth and our worth
They told us there's no alternative
to taking so much more that we could ever give back
But let's listen to the language of longing
the story of the life force calls us back to belonging

Slow down, look up, go outside
We're all natives who've been de-tribalized
Crashed, and we've trashed the land
Depressed, alone, with grasping hands
While all the wild world waves its branches, wings, & clouds
like flags to try and win us back
Respect for the endless spiral is all that we lack
If only we believed there was something else called *Possible*
to welcome us back into the largest story

Earthsong of the wolf
Oceansong of the whale
Starlight on snow and sacred stones
All sending us their stories
Conspiring as hawks and waves
storms and waterfalls
Will we turn and learn to count
our future selves among them all?

Change the story to one of awakening
The great turning of our time
Turn from deathly entertainment
and salvation in the sky
Welcome the pain of empathy--
compassion means *to suffer with*
The homeless standing there, dying before our eyes
The seeds left crying under pavements beneath these toxic skies
We made this land an aircraft carrier
an armed satellite
Tanks of free trade smashing all life
All for the story of empires and kings
but life sings out in memories we can't outrun
The path we're on is burning

our destruction's almost done

We're members of this planet,
not its monsters, or its masters
We can stop being tourists in our animal bodies
drop the spectator pose
Know that all our depression's been mis-diagnosed
Return to the home we remember
in the compass of our bones

What is the calculus of hope?
The geometry of gratitude?
What's the algebra of all my relations?
How much for the first spring flower?
How much for a blizzard in a drought now?
How do I measure poetry?
How do we fall in love with the whole holy world
shedding armor like daisy petals
'cos she loves us--
And all the kings horses
And all the king's men
Can't stop a billion hearts beating
like an infinite spring
When we tell the story
where we walk away from the king.

~ Twenty-One ~

TAKE BACK THE NIGHT

My mother always told me not to out alone at night. Not to wear short skirts, or go to parties without parents there, to wear panties, not to leave the shades open, not even a crack. I thought she was paranoid. I didn't know then that just because you're anxious doesn't mean they're aren't monsters out to get you.

My mother's father was a monster. He incested her, and me, her sister, all my girl cousins, and he brutalized his wife. He was told by his world that we were his possessions. She never told me any of this, except that she remembered incest, in therapy, at the age of 75.

Five months ago, my mother died. In the process of her dying, she fell through the ice of her life long secret, trapped in a three day long nightmare calling out from her tiny nursing home bed: "Papa! No, Papa, No!" Like that, over and over. Just her and me in that tiny cell together, and my father, pretending to sleep, and her father, deeply present, possibly the most solid energy in that room. And "No, Papa, No!" was her mantra for three days and nights while I tried to hold her tight, tried to winch her out of the ice water, tried to tie him down, tried to interrupt the possession.

She was 94 years old. She lay there, semi-conscious, her tiny face a fist that couldn't hit, her bared teeth fierce and her hands fluttering like wild birds that had gotten trapped inside the held-back breath of that space.

Nurses and aides moved through the room, moved her body, moved around me, where I knelt, frozen, for days. I lay with her in that narrow bed and whispered in her good ear for hours at a time: "Let's go, Mama, we can just leave, right now. We can just walk right out of this room. I'm here. We can go, together."

But I had ceased to register on her radar; I was gone. All she could do was thrash and struggle, panting. It was just her and him. It was just Me and him. It was just him.

After the second day, I called my friend, the Jewish mystic healer, to come and clear the evil out of that room, to exorcise my grandfather from my mother's ancient dying body.

That day, nothing changed. Her bared-teeth terror mask froze deeper, and the panting of "No Papa no" became her breathing. That night I slept on the floor in the space between my parents' narrow beds like a loyal golden retriever, except I didn't sleep. I lay there, triggered backwards in time. I couldn't stop crying, shaking. The strongest person in that room was my Zayda, and he'd been dead since 1965.

The next day, the healer came back, and this time she sent me out of the room. When I returned, an hour or 2 later, Mama's teeth were unclenched, her grimace gone. Her wild bird hands were still. She was breathing deeply, asleep. She was almost gone. "Don't touch her", the healer warned, She's very close now. Don't do anything to bring her back." She was shrunken and shining and peaceful.

And when she died, the next morning, the rabbi came and wove defensive spells, and the Chevra Kadisha, the holy Jewish burial society, dressed her in white, tied white silken knots in the symbols of Hebrew letters of Heavenly protection, around her wrists, her throat, her ankles.

And I brought her home to me, to lie with me forever, buried her 40 feet from my door on my mountain, and Adenoi, the Jewish warrior god came along to guard her graveside. He's still there, protecting her with his flaming sword, and we are learning to tolerate each other's fundamentalism. His son, my grandfather, is banished forever from our bodies. We sent him, my mother, her god, my goddess and I, away, into the airless depths of outer space, far from the tender flesh of innocent girls.

She is safe now. Safe to the night. Safe to walk alone, to dress how she pleases, safe to open the curtains wide, stand in front of all the night windows.

Dead, she is safe.

I am a survivor, of incest. Of rape. Of Patriarchy. A survivor of the catcalls of rape, the vampire gaze of rape, the relentless fear of rape that all women know and most men do not see. How do women survive the paralyzing fear of rape, the invisible secret that haunts our days? I want to tie white silk ribbons around our hearts and all the tender places where we ache with what we know.

Last year, I was invited to speak on a panel about rape. This was on a morning radio show, at my local progressive radio station. It was a call-in show. There were 5 of us. The moderator began with some data. The numbers of women who are raped, the non-reporting. When it was my turn, I corrected her grammar, the agent-less passive. "Women are raped. Women are battered." You English professors know what I'm talking about. "Women are raped by men", I said.

We talked for 30 more minutes, about the horrors of rape, women's fear of rape, rape culture. Afterwards, the phone lines lit up, and the first 9 calls were from men who were furious at me for saying that men rape women, outraged that I had dared to state the obvious, and upset their morning coffee or yoga, or whatever. They insisted over and over that *they* do not rape. One said, *No wonder you get raped.* This was KGNU, progressive bastion of Boulder. It was 8:30 in the freaking morning. Who were these guys?

This night is about women's voices. I know that not all men rape, but that doesn't matter much to me, cos the big secret of rape culture is alive and hardy in patriarchy. We swim in their entitlement and our own hopelessness. We drown in toxic images of brutal masculinity and victimized femininity. We have ignorant legislators and right wing backlashers and left wing supremacists who only deepen women's hell.

All women are afraid of being raped, of being murdered if they resist rape, of being blamed or disbelieved if they report rape. We worry about our future promised rapes. It's a stone in the belly, a shard in the brain, and yet we're taught to abandon ourselves in order to protect male comfort levels. We don't speak of it to them, to you, the good men. But what about the not-so-good men, of whom there are way too many? If you're too nice, you lead them on. If you're too honest, you risk violence. Either way, you're a bitch. We try to stand on thinnest ice, to not fall through.

Patriarchy. The massive power differential between us, the sinister forms uncoiling, the relentless pattern of gender roles in our society. We live in a culture, in a world steeped in the domination of women. We women circle the cold sucking drain of misogyny. Misogyny: the hatred of women. You've heard the story of the battle: the one who screamed and fought back and got away; the one who was roofied and did not remember. The stories of the battles surround us, but this is The Battle of the Story. History paves over the fear women suffer. Who's gonna name the terror, who will nar-rate the dark streets and corridors, the beds and bars of battle?

I say it: patriarchy is alive and thriving. It's the very real stage on which we all perform rape culture. It is the idea that a man has a right to have sex with a woman, regardless of her desires. It's the fact that his rights trump hers', or she just has no rights. Or she just has no voice, no place in the gender script except as an object to be desired and conquered and owned. This sense of being owed sex is everywhere. We owe them. They have a right. To us.

Because they need it, because life is hard and we are soft. Be-cause they bought us a drink, because rape culture keeps them in a constant state of aggression and arousal, and because we are deliv-ered to them as sexual delivery systems, objects, caricatures shaken like a red flag at a bull to slake those out of control hungers. Our bodies plastered over every screen, over every street, over every pornographic ad, over their eyeballs.

The invalidity of the word NO. The danger of the family home. The workplace, the party, the college campus.

To win the battle of the story, women must become both credi-ble and audible.

At the heart of the struggle of Feminism is a passion and duty to name and re-name the world. To resist the story that women are not reliable witnesses to our own lives. To say that for all of history, the truth was never our property.

And all the uncountable generations, the millennia of women who weren't allowed into the laboratory or the library or the con-versation or the revolution, or even the category called human cry out to us tonight to march, to change the world, again, even if it's just in a parking lot, because this is *symbolic*, a *ritual*. We march, we dare, we fight back. Because this is a war. Rape is a war. It may be the oldest war. I depend now upon younger women to say what you need to say and be who you want to be and go where you choose to go. Proudly. Safely. Even dangerously, because what could be more dangerous than our silence? What could be more deadly to rape culture than our voices?

This one night of women's voices in a world where space opens up for men, shuts down for women. Where power is expressed in discourse and physical violence, and the world is still organized to silence and annihilate us.

We work so hard to rise up out of that annihilation. My Mama worked so hard. She clarified her story in the fragile beaker of her body. She crossed the threshold of alchemy and became pure gold. She did this for me, and for all her female relations. I believe she did it for All of Us, and so I call her in to march beside us tonight, in our symbolic ritual, in that parking lot, because she would be proud to be a subject of this story in our battle, as we dare to take back the night.

Thanks for listening.

Spring, 2015

~ Twenty-Two ~

ATONEMENT

The sun is a wheel writing time in the sky
Autumn smell of leaves and dust
it's Rosh Hashanah watching us
The season of atonement comes
appeasing all the homeless ones
my people as the Chosen Ones
wrestling with god for reconciliation
never having had a nation
chased through history from home to home
Jews believe in the will to atone
Believe that at -one -moment
everything can change
oppression and victimhood rearranged
Forgiveness.

'Cos we've been railroaded and scapegoated
framed and shamed and blamed for 2,000 years
We came to expect the unexpected
nightmares of a race collected and
sent off on trains to be ashes forever
extinguished.

But some of us got away

I grew up among those European refugees
barely saved from the flames and talking strange
with numbers in blue
tattooed *Jew* on their flesh
like expiration dates
They came to the states to learn to be white
where their kids learned to kiss suffering good night
and their kids' kids learned to sleep with mistrust
the ashes calling and the dust

It's inherited — PTSD, post traumatic stress disorder
Trust no one outside the gates of your ghetto's borders
And maybe after World War 2
they should've given Germany to the Jews
instead of this 2,000 year migration route
Because a victim mentality pervades Jewish life
& it keeps us turning on the knife edge of survival
The only home we know's the bible so
we turned our fears inward
made Israel a victim state
and the U.S. media seals the fate
of a gated community, offers immunity
by feeding us one- sided images
of Palestinian suicide bombers
and Palestinian terrorism

But the victims in Israel aren't the Jews
if you choose to accuse anybody of terrorism
check out the hardware of military imperialism
Zionism used to mean just simply going home to Zion
but now Zionism means

endless aggressive expansion
and violence in defense of endless aggressive expansion
And there's an irony to this kind of Zionism
it's internalized anti-semitism
It means you believe we're meant to be
foreigners in every country but one
and that one has the most guns
and crazy people running it
Jews in Israel live to protect a homeland
but
there's a disconnect
in thinking a homeland could ever save you
the next time they come to enslave you
Like a homeland could ever save African people,
Native American people,
any indigenous people on land
from a racist conquerors with a gun in his hand
Look at Palestine

The deepening catastrophe of Palestine
The bible says its the fire next time
but that's this time
don't you see?
'Cos the right wing Christians in power in this country
love Israel
A military state
right in the middle of all that hate
Its like a giant U.S. army base
squatting atop all those oil pipelines
It's where the George Bushes keep armageddon ticking
keep the born again Christians licking their lips and tripping
imagining themselves saved forever in Paradise
so the Jews and the Arabs are set up to fight the final battle

Bring on the holy apocalypse!
'cos the book of revelation insists
And meanwhile, pump up the oil pressure
cos the corporations got to measure the treasure
They want to steal all that oil
from underneath the Arab people's soil
so the toiling of racism continues to boil
cooking the bones
of all the outsiders just trying to get home

The elites set us up as scapegoats again
for oil and war and armageddon
Now we're officially the chosen ones
chosen by the US government to wield the guns
When will we learn?
Maybe next time
and here comes the eternal victim line —
They all want us dead
says my mother's voice inside my head
They all want you all dead
repeat the media talking heads
So, here's Apache helicopters, U.S. bulldozers
a government that's just for you
all of this and an army too
And watch Jews toughen
from those meek folks herded onto trains
set up to be the brains, the heartless enemy
on the front lines of the Middle East
holocaust
What's the cost
of turning into the oppressor?

Dark eyes at the barbed wire
shift
from the Warsaw Ghetto to Ramallah
Each year at Passover, Jews say
Next year in Jeruselem
No way!
Next year in Jeruselem *we'll* be destroying lives and homes?
We'll build the next camps?
Jews will be the next drones
to lock step march into the future of the final war?
Are you sure we said that?
I didn't say that

I try to understand but who can understand?
Just put down your guns and share the land
Governments thrive by driving our fears up to screech
In the US and in Israel its time to impeach these
testosterone soaked patriarchs in power
because the people want peace

So, turn your grizzled cheek and see
the connection of all the meek
people manipulated by the powers that be
And let your power be to Free
the earth forever from disconnection
pissed off gods and shadow projections
On this holy day, just learn to trust
as the golden leaves of Rosh Hashanah
crumble into dust

Fall, 2003

~ Twenty-Three ~

ZAPATISTA

Zappatista

Who owns history?
What do we mean when we say Revolution?
We march and we want it to change
we want the world saved so that we can go home
but it's always too soon to go home

History isn't an army marching forward
it's drips of water changing stone
Hope is a door
or the vision of a door
While we wave the flag and clutch the cross
older symbols arise to the south

There are Mayan poets in southern Mexico
writing radical chapters of history in their masks
in their mountains
Imagine an army melting into a jungle of poetry and theater
Rebellion means telling other stories
Outside of history books they're changing history
What does it mean to be one person who hasn't been conquered?

When every other revolution
was about seizing power from the state
they turn their backs on the state and face instead
the sacred details of their days
Forget about reorganizing this nightmare
They walk slowly asking questions
a solidarity movement their indigenous weapon
Instead of a world of us and them
they say they live in a world of *two we's*
There's this we
here, in this circle, in this room
and there's the larger We
every other person out there on the spiral

They carry seeds under siege
and we —
— the largest We
spiral outwards
from the intention of their unshelled hearts
We are their shield and their witness
the fire and the word
and the present, wide open
in defense of hope

From the edges of the shadows
with the power of the powerless
imagine them
Tear the chains off your brain
and find a way
to join the dream that will set history
free.

2001

~ Twenty-Four ~

A WAY THROUGH

The philodendron
uncoils
winding along in air
Climbed the wall and got stuck in her dance at a horizontal beam
there, above the southeast kitchen window
I find her jammed, affixed magically to the recycled maple
tongue and groove
Tightly she fed, ferocious in her push
terminus still palest green where I yanked it gently free
tattooing her way along the final route
she sent out roots to hold her tight
Feeling like scouts to search
for a way through

Wall-bending strength of this undaunted vine
pasted to once-living hardwood cousin
giant caterpillar rolling through time
blindly leaning in, pressing with the force of a mountain range
silently crushing all resistance from its dreaming heart.
Forward only.
Just this force
thrusting with her blind green hands

Only
this

And the great tower of Texas excavated cactus
kidnapped in a Toyota, born to live in this room
reaching at last past the ceiling, through
crumpling at the tip
inside a purpose that insists past the crisis
The hustle of the push
rocket thrusted at the cusp
bump butting bionic sword
soaring inside a green wattage
spanking the obstacle, insistent
dispatched to the job of life's determination
with a moxie beyond human
Film heroes pale beside this level of authority
staggering to my morning idle.
For years she's been a mute gangbuster humming life! Life!
Sighing softly between the teeth that run
the length of her serpent rising body as she fought
inside a thunderous assault
resounding down and up her tree trunk
Sparks from her thorns rage through my sleep
bother my dreams just upstairs
as she muscled her way through
Through! A battle cry
Her green sword roaring to batter
And every finger unfolding since she hit that ceiling
born bent with the shove and kick of mission
inherited here for this vengeance
on a dead pine ceiling that is also a floor
and only an obstacle
unleashing beneath an old carpet

unsleeping rebel hammer set in motion, forever

And I, breathless witness
can only search through books to describe to the day
in my rest, it's opposite
Planted and reaching all round me
and so, nature is not idle.
Nature is mapped within
set to a task that unfolds in sacred sovereignty
whether we watch or not
A kinetic intelligence
a competence that says to the men in suits: This is industry.
To the politicos: This is activism!
Who's unsung might lifts whole houses with a single green fin-
ger

I'm thinking about fractivists
about witches created to speak for the land
and the ceiling we face in our sleep is the government,
is banks, words on paper
the guns and police of the corporate industrial waste society
And I pray for the vehemence
the Push
the green vigor of plants
to open our hearts and eyes
and infuse us with their inspiration
To push through every thwarting form
only to insist on Life
that must continue.

~ Twenty-Five ~

THOUGHT CRIMES

Beyond the rate of data
the inconceivably small or distant
nuclei of cells, HTML code, quarks
beneath the god-function of naming
saffron tinted cactus flowers
lift themselves up into July's heat

Unspeaking testament
to an other eloquence
curating this barnacle brain
with your fierce chisel
Authority wants to replace the world
with itself
Ventriloquist
resist clamping the words in my head
to the page to shut them up
I have lines inside me
like a string of guiding lights
guilty of thought crimes

Certainty's the booby prize
mere habit mutes me

Baffled
beside the vast vernacular of nature
While waves stroke plastic beaches
names and processes I don't know
swim past my baited fishing pole

I know how words work
like boys know how machines work
Unhooked from the digital drumbeat
and surroundings once removed
yet
always we're walking on words
— the floor the walls the doors, *words* —
We got souls to save, worlds to conquer
words to slide against each other
burning with too-big brains
but the world burns faster

To be a slingshot instead of a lockbox
To cleanse the gateways
& let the world pass
To not know what time it is every day
to not know what day it is all the time
To not. To knot.
To spin the knots to parachute
To knot the string
and call it Shakespeare
— call it God
The thing you touch with your fingers
direct communion, like Braille
participation
like worms, waves, wolves

To slide the awful story from my shoulders
discover the cool peace of rootlets
calm dissolve of this land
drenched in life-giving rains
offering
everything
Just watch the spider walk on air
silver intellect on a crystal page
To be a spider, born with all I need to know
and a short condensed journey of purpose
To be a molecule of water roaring home
just one tiny piece of that unity
only clean-cut sand, stone's future
or that image of the earth seen from space
You are here.

Wagging this long ineffable tail
full of screeching peacock pronouncements
failures of grammar
babble of beauty
Touching a world that's
the roaring heart of a great bonfire
blaze drives me back but
i resist retreat to human
These pockets full of heart shaped rocks
proof that the land loves me back
and questions, unconquered
coming through
like a thrillion beeping messages
a stammer of imperfect speech
Seasons redeem me while
Kali surrounds me
with the ten thousand things

I dissolve in Her mouth
torrential silence
unspoken
as light

The only word to the butterfly, *nectar*
The only truth to the river, *down.*

Oak Chezar is a revolutionary, a performance artist, a dyke, and a writer who has been creating and performing with Vox Feminista for 25 years. Excessive quantities of higher education prepared her to take great notes. Excessive quantities of rage keep her going. Performing standup comedy as Vampyra, her alter ego, keeps her out of prison, and the eclectic glories of A.D.H.D. make her a fascinating conversationalist. Oak's other art form is the pleasure and beauty of a simple life; she models alternative lifestyle as a genre of service: showing U.S.ians how to live joyfully with less stuff. From her hand built, recycled straw bale house, she wanders the mountains, memorizing patterns. Whilst working for the decimation of industrial civilization she carries water.

CPSIA information can be obtained
at www.ICGtesting.com
Printed in the USA
FSHW011701111119
63982FS